D1626834

Usborne Beginners
Romans

Katie Daynes
Illustrated by Adam Larkum
Designed by Katrina Fearn

Romans consultant: Aude Doody, PhD, University of Cambridge
Reading consultant: Alison Kelly, University of Surrey Roehampton

Contents

In Roman times

The first Romans lived in the city of Rome over a thousand years ago. They had a strong army and took over many countries.

Every Roman town had a
big open space where people met,
heard the latest news and went shopping.

3

People of Rome

In Rome, there were rich people, poor people and slaves. The most powerful person was the emperor.

The emperor ruled over all Roman lands.

Men called senators gave him advice.

This coin shows the head of Augustus, the first emperor.

He won many battles and made Rome more peaceful.

People captured in a battle were often sold as slaves.

Rich Romans bought slaves to do hard work for them.

Some masters made their slaves work in their storerooms.

Other masters made their slaves cook meals for them.

Once a year, slaves and masters changed places for the day.

5

At home

In Roman towns, most people rented rooms.
Only rich Romans could afford houses.

Poor people
rented rooms
on the top floor.

Richer people
had big rooms
lower down.

There were
often shops at
street level.

Romans didn't use wallpaper. They
just painted pictures on their walls.

This is a Roman wall painting of a villa.
Villas were big houses where the rich lived.

Rich Romans had mosaics on their floors.

A worker spread plaster on the floor.

He made a pattern out of small tiles.

On the streets

The streets of Rome were often packed with people. Vehicles were only allowed at night.

At dawn, street cleaners swept the streets and sellers arrived with their goods.

By noon, the streets were very busy. Rich Romans were carried in boxes called litters.

At night, the vehicles arrived. People carried torches because there were no street lights.

Many Romans didn't have a kitchen, so they ate in cafés.

They got their drinking water from public fountains.

This mosaic shows musicians playing to people on the street.

What to wear

Most Roman men and women dressed up in long, flowing pieces of material.

Everyone wore a simple cloth tunic.

Women wore a dress over their tunic.

Sometimes they wore a big shawl too.

Rich women had slaves to help them do their hair and make-up.

They put chalk on their face and painted their lips red.

Important men draped a huge piece of material over their tunic. It was called a toga.

This is a statue of a Roman man wearing a toga.

Only the emperor was allowed to dress all in purple.

Going shopping

People did their shopping in local shops or at a market.

This shop sold olive oil.

This one sold material.

People bought pottery here.

Food sellers made fresh food each day at the back of their shops.

Bakers ground wheat to make flour.

They made dough with the flour...

...then baked the dough to make bread.

This carving shows a butcher chopping meat in his shop.

At the markets, people sold fresh fruit and vegetables from the countryside.

Farming

Most Roman food came from farms.

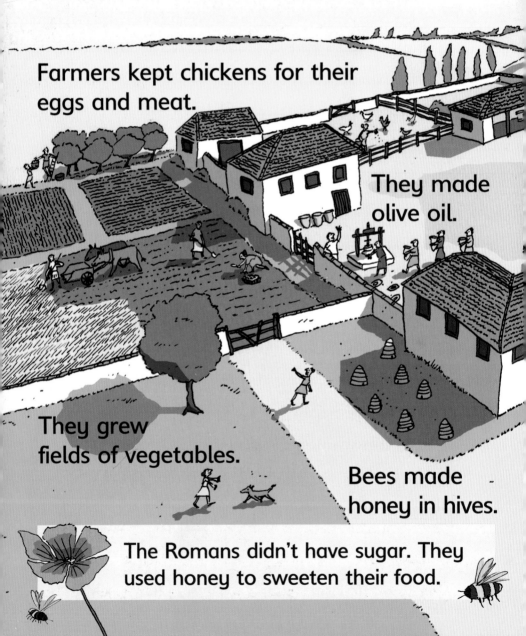

Farmers kept chickens for their eggs and meat.

They made olive oil.

They grew fields of vegetables.

Bees made honey in hives.

The Romans didn't have sugar. They used honey to sweeten their food.

Sheep were kept for
their milk, wool
and meat.

Pig meat
was very
popular.

Farmers grew grapes to make juice and wine.

They picked
the grapes...

...squashed
out the juice...

...and stored
it in jars.

15

Banquets

Rich people invited friends to huge evening meals called banquets.

Guests arrived and took their sandals off by the door.

Slaves washed their feet, then led them to the banquet room.

The guests lay down on couches and had their hands washed.

Slaves brought in fancy foods and lots of wine.

Guests ate with their fingers, straight from the serving plates.

They were entertained with music and dancing.

Stuffed dormice and peacock brains were served as treats.

At the baths

In Roman times, people didn't wash at home. They went to the public baths.

First they went into the steam room.

Then they soaked in the hot room.

They relaxed in the warm room...

...before a dip in the cold pool outside.

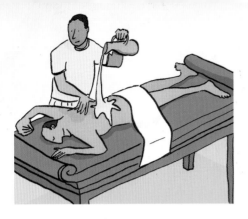

Romans washed with oil. Slaves rubbed it onto their skin.

Then they scraped it off with a stick. The dirt came off too.

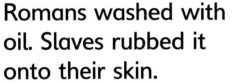

Roman public toilets looked like this. People sat in a line on the holes.

Everyone dressed the same way at the baths. They all wore nothing!

Gods and goddesses

The Romans used to worship gods and goddesses. Here are some important ones.

Jupiter was the king of the gods.

He married the powerful goddess Juno.

Their son, Mars, was god of war.

Diana was the goddess of hunting.

Mercury took messages for Jupiter.

Venus was the goddess of love.

On holy days, people went to temples with gifts for the gods.

Priests killed animals for the gods. Then they ate the meat.

Some Roman temples still stand today. This one is missing its roof.

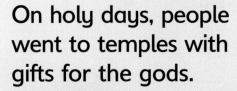

Every spring, the Romans had a party to celebrate Flora, the goddess of flowers.

Building power

The Romans built many amazing things, such as temples, ships and aqueducts.

Aqueducts were bridges that carried water into towns. Their arches were hard to build.

Builders made a curved wood frame.

They built bricks around the frame.

Then they took the frame away.

The Romans built sailing ships to collect food and material from other countries.

They also built fast ships for sea battles. Men attacked their enemies with balls of fire.

Inside the ships, men sat in rows and pulled on oars to make the ship go faster.

At school

Only the sons of rich Romans went to school in Roman times.

They were taught to read and write.

They used a metal pen to scratch words onto a wax tablet.

Then they smoothed the wax and tried writing again.

Older students wrote in ink on paper made from plants.

They wrote speeches and learned how to act them out.

All students learned how to count. Romans wrote numbers using letters, like this.

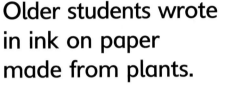

1 = I   5 = V   9 = IX

2 = II   6 = VI   10 = X

3 = III   7 = VII   11 = XI

4 = IV   8 = VIII   12 = XII

Girls didn't go to school. They got married at a very young age.

In the army

The Romans had a very powerful army made up of thousands of soldiers.

The soldiers spent days marching to new battles.

Each evening, they built a camp where they could rest.

They broke through the wall around their enemy's town.

Then they marched in, using their shields like a tortoise's shell.

Roman soldiers looked like this when they went into battle.

Games and races

For a fun day out, Romans went to the games or to the races.

The games took place in a big round stadium.

The day began with music, dancing and circus tricks.

Then slaves called gladiators fought each other.

Many gladiators were killed in fights at the games.

28

Sometimes there were animal hunts at the games too. This Roman wall painting shows a man hunting a lion.

At chariot races, men rode in carts pulled by horses.

They raced around a track. It was very fast and dangerous.

Glossary of Roman words

Here are some of the words in this book you might not know. This page tells you what they mean.

 emperor – the man who ruled over Rome and all Roman lands.

 slave – a person who works for no money. Rich Romans owned slaves.

 mosaic – a picture or pattern on the floor made of little stones or tiles.

 litter – a big box for rich Romans to travel in. They were carried by slaves.

 aqueduct – a bridge built to carry drinking water into a Roman town.

 gladiator – a man who had to fight at the games. He was usually a slave.

 chariot – a cart pulled by two, four, six or sometimes even eight horses.

Websites to visit

If you have a computer, you can find out more about the ancient Romans on the Internet. On the Usborne Quicklinks website there are links to four fun websites.

Website 1 – See pictures of how ancient Rome looks today.

Website 2 – Play a Roman bath game.

Website 3 – Race against the clock to match Roman and English numbers.

Website 4 – Print out seven fun activities about Roman life.

To visit these websites, go to **www.usborne-quicklinks.com** and type the keywords "beginners romans". Then click on the link for the website you want to visit. Before you use the Internet, look at the safety guidelines inside the back cover of this book and ask an adult to read them with you.

Index

Acknowledgements

Photographic manipulation by Emma Julings

Photo credits
The publishers are grateful to the following for permission to reproduce material:
© **Alamy** (Frank Miesnikowicz) 21; © **Copyright The British Museum** 4;
© **Corbis** (Gianni Dagli Orti) title page, (Mimmo Jodice) 7 & 31, (Archivo Iconografico, S.A.) 9 & 13,
(Araldo de Luca) 11, (John and Dallas Heaton) 22, (Charles & Josette Lenars) 26-27,
(Ruggero Vanni) 29; © **Robert Harding** (Michael Jenner) 19

Every effort has been made to trace and acknowledge ownership of copyright. If any rights have
been omitted, the publishers offer to rectify this in any subsequent editions following notification.

Internet safety rules

- Ask your parent's or guardian's permission before you connect to the Internet.

- When you are on the Internet, never tell anyone your full name, address or telephone number, and ask an adult before you give your email address.

- If a website asks you to log in or register by typing your name or email address, ask an adult's permission first.

- If you do receive an email from someone you don't know, tell an adult and do not reply to the email.

Notes for parents or guardians

The websites described in this book are regularly reviewed and the links in Usborne Quicklinks are updated. However, the content of a website may change at any time and Usborne Publishing is not responsible, and does not accept liability, for the content or availability of any website other than its own, or for any exposure to harmful, offensive or inaccurate material which may appear on the Web. We recommend that children are supervised while on the Internet, that they do not use Internet Chat Rooms and that you use Internet filtering software to block unsuitable material. Please ensure that your children follow the safety guidelines printed above. For more information, see the "Net Help" area on the Usborne Quicklinks website at **www.usborne-quicklinks.com**